DATE			

Sound

Graham Peacock

Thomson Learning · New York

Books in the series:

SOUND • LIGHT
HEAT • MATERIALS • WATER • ELECTRICITY

First published in the
United States in 1993 by
Thomson Learning
115 Fifth Avenue
New York, NY 10003

First published in 1993 by
Wayland (Publishers) Ltd.

Copyright © 1993 by Wayland (Publishers) Ltd.

U.S. revision copyright © 1993 Thomson Learning

Cataloging-in-Publication Data applied for

ISBN: 1-56847-074-6

Printed in Italy

Acknowledgments
The publishers would like to thank the following for allowing their
pictures to be used in this book: Chapel Studios 21; Korg (UK) *cover
(bottom right);* Natural History Photographic Agency *cover (top);* Tony
Stone Worldwide 22; Wayland Picture Library 28; Zefa 11, 29. All
commissioned photographs are from the Wayland Picture Library (Zul
Mukhida). All artwork is by Tony de Saulles.

Contents

Words that appear in **bold** are explained in the glossary on page 30.

Hearing sound

Have you ever wondered what sound is? It is not something that you can see or touch, but a sound is made every time something on earth moves, even if it is too quiet for human ears to hear. Sound does not exist on its own, but all sounds come from a **source.** In this book you will explore how a sound travels from its source into your ears, and how it is understood by your brain.

Do you need two ears?

1 Sit in a chair and blindfold your eyes.

2 Ask your friends to make sounds by clicking their fingers or clapping once. They should make the noises near to the ground, high up, in front and behind you.

3 Point to the place where the sound is coming from.

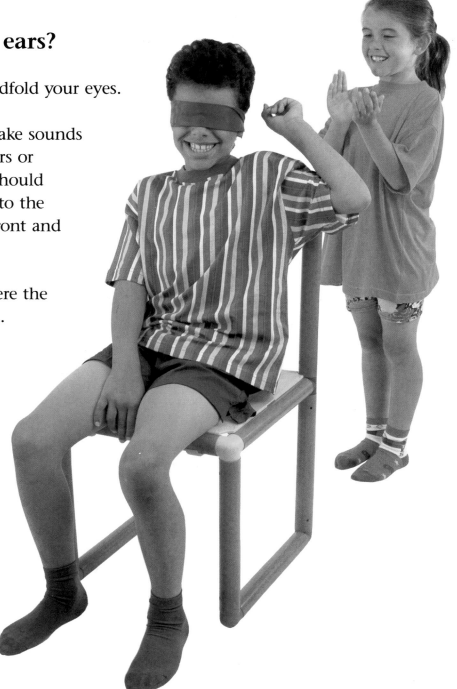

4 Cover one ear and do the same as before. Now you may find it harder to tell where the sounds come from.

Who has got the best hearing?

Plan a test to see which of your friends has the best hearing.

You will have to find a way of making the same quiet sound for each test, or the test will not be fair.

You can tell where a sound comes from because the ear closer to the sound hears it louder and just before the other ear. If both ears hear the sound at the same time, then the sound is either directly in front of or behind you.

Most animals can hear, but not all animals have ears on their heads.

Grasshoppers detect sound through their legs.

Fish have ears inside their heads. They do not need openings on their heads to let sounds in. That is because sound travels so well in water that it easily reaches the ear.

Crocodiles cover each ear with a scaly flap when they are swimming. They open the flaps when they are on land.

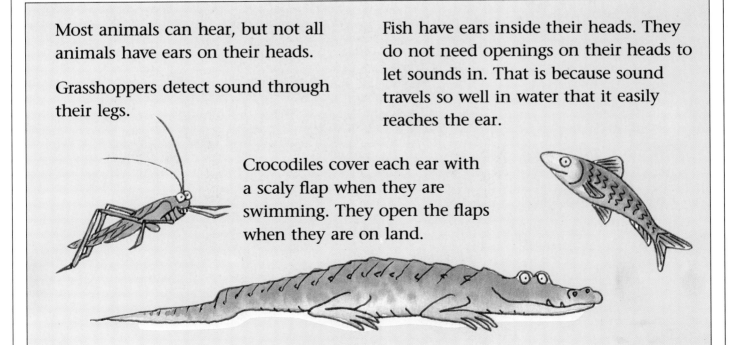

What is inside your ear?

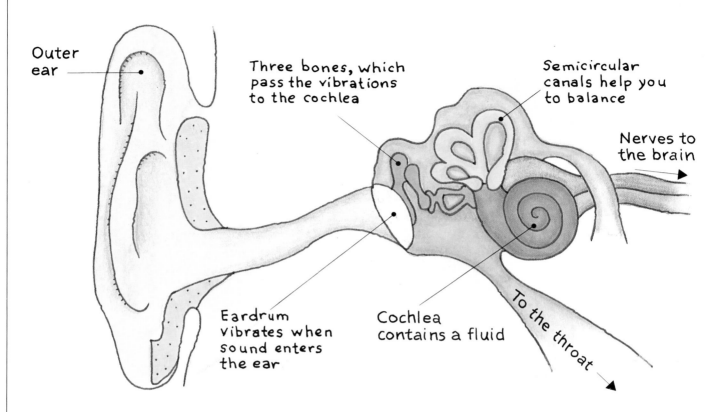

Outer ear

Three bones, which pass the vibrations to the cochlea

Semicircular canals help you to balance

Nerves to the brain

Eardrum vibrates when sound enters the ear

Cochlea contains a fluid

To the throat

Make a model ear

You will need:

- a short fat tube
- a piece of plastic wrap
- a rubber band
- cardboard or paper
- Scotch tape
- a scrap of aluminum foil
- a flashlight or sunshine

1 Make a cone out of the paper or cardboard and tape it onto the tube.

2 Cover the bottom of the tube with the piece of plastic wrap. Hold it tightly in place with a rubber band.

3 Stick a piece of foil onto the plastic wrap, using the Scotch tape.

4 Talk into the cardboard cone. Feel the air making the plastic wrap vibrate. This is how your ear and **eardrum** work.

5 Shine a flashlight on the foil (or use sunlight) to make a reflection on a wall. See how the reflected spot of light changes as you talk into the "ear."

Did you know?

The stirrup bone in your ear is the smallest bone in your body. When it vibrates, it presses on the liquid in the **cochlea.** This produces tiny amounts of electricity, which pass along the nerves to your brain.

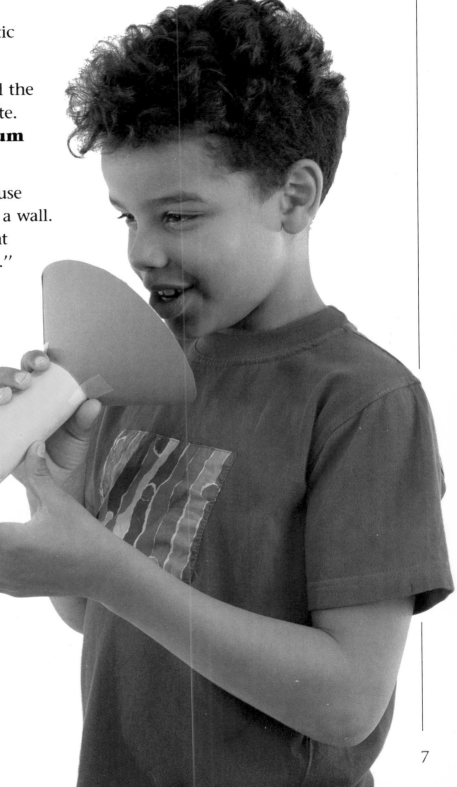

Vibrations

All sounds are caused by **vibrations** in the air. When something moves back and forth very quickly, we say it vibrates.

Feel the vibration

You will need:

- a piece of paper
- a comb
- a blown-up balloon

1 Fold the comb inside the piece of paper and hold it lightly against your lips. Make a "coo" sound. Feel your lips tingle as the paper vibrates.

2 Hold a balloon against your lips and make a "coo" sound. Feel the balloon vibrate.

Tuning fork vibrations

You will need:

a tuning fork   an eraser   a box or can

1 Tap the **tuning fork** on the eraser.

2 Look carefully and you will see it vibrate.

3 Touch the vibrating tuning fork with your fingernail. You will feel it vibrate.

4 Make the sound louder by standing the vibrating tuning fork on a box or can.

Traveling vibrations

The hammer hits the bell.   The air vibrates.   Your eardrum vibrates.

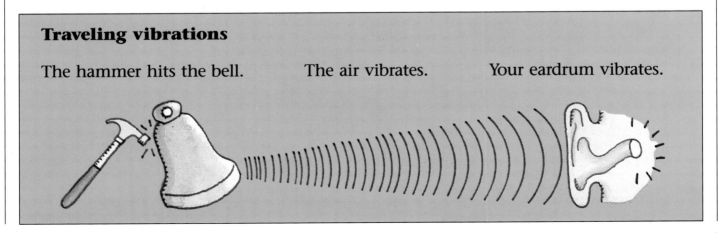

Guess the sound

Which sounds can people recognize?

You will need:

small numbered containers with lids   small objects such as nails, coins, dry beans, pebbles, or sand

1 Put an object in each container.

2 Shake each container near a friend. See if your friend can guess what is in each one from the sounds it makes.

3 Figure out which sound is easiest to identify and which is most difficult. Make a record of your results.

Which recorded sounds can people recognize?

Use a battery-operated tape recorder to record different sounds. Say a number out loud before you make each recording, and write down what you have recorded.

When people hear a baby crying, they know that it is hungry or tired.

1 Record some very quiet sounds very close up. Make each recording last at least four seconds.

2 Give people a quiz. Play back your recording and see which sounds they can guess.

True or false?

1 Crocodiles hear through their legs.
2 One of your ears sometimes hears a sound before the other ear.
3 The eardrum is the smallest bone in your body.
4 Your ear changes sound into tiny amounts of electricity.
5 Grasshoppers have ears all over their bodies.
6 You hear a sound when something makes the air vibrate.

These topics are discussed on pages 4–11. Answers are on page 32.

Sound waves

Sound travels in **sound waves.** Sound waves move like water waves. Have you ever watched a seagull floating on the sea? It stays in the same place, but is carried up on the tops of the waves and down in the dips on either side.

Waves are made when a material such as air or water is pushed together in some places and pulled apart in others. The air or water stays in the same place, like the seagull, but the waves move through it.

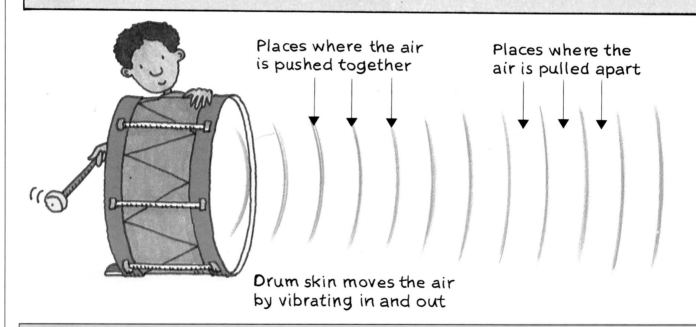

Places where the air is pushed together

Places where the air is pulled apart

Drum skin moves the air by vibrating in and out

Wavelength

The distance between two waves is called the wavelength.

The wavelength of a sound affects its **pitch.**

High-pitched sounds, such as a scream, have a short wavelength.

Low-pitched sounds, such as a grunt, have a long wavelength.

Slinky springs

You can buy Slinky springs from a toy shop. They let you see waves traveling.

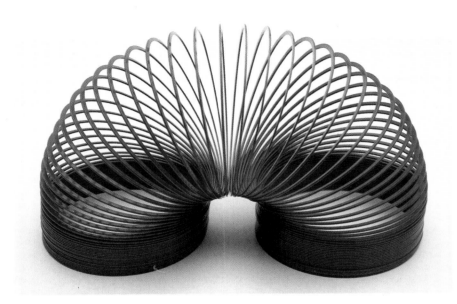

1 Stretch your Slinky spring.

2 Tap one end once. Watch the vibration travel in a wave to the other end.

3 Notice that if you tap the spring in the middle, the vibrations will travel away in both directions.

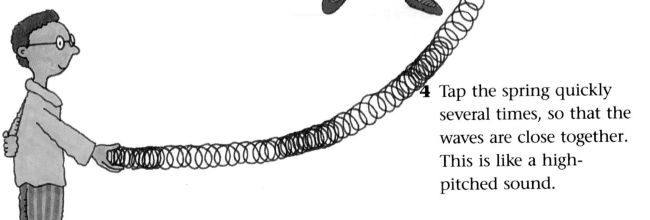

4 Tap the spring quickly several times, so that the waves are close together. This is like a high-pitched sound.

5 Now tap the spring more slowly, so that the waves are farther apart. This is like a low-pitched sound.

13

Sound through the air

Does sound travel faster than light?

1 Ask a friend to go at least one hundred large steps away from you.

2 Get her or him to make a noise by banging two sticks together.

3 Do you see your friend hit the sticks together and then hear the sound, or do you hear the sound first?

Sound travels about one mile in five seconds. Light travels nearly one million miles in five seconds. This is why, from a long way off, you see the sticks bang together before you hear the sound they make. It is also why, in a storm, you see lightning before you hear thunder, even though they happen at the same time.

The loudest sound ever heard by people was when the volcano Krakatoa erupted in 1883. Krakatoa is in Indonesia; the explosion was heard 3,000 miles away in Australia.

Quiz

How long would it have taken the sound from Krakatoa to reach Australia?

A Three seconds.
B About four hours.
C Two days.

The answer is on page 32.

Why do sounds echo?

Stand about forty large steps away from a tall blank wall in a quiet place. Clap your hands, or bang two blocks together. Listen for the **echo.**

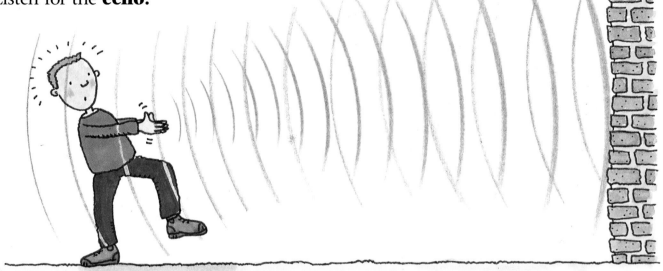

Sound waves bounce back from solid surfaces. You cannot hear the echoes in small rooms because sound bounces back off the walls too quickly to hear the echo separately.

It is silent in space because there is no air for sound waves to travel through. This astronaut cannot hear the noisiest rocket coming.

Hearing better in air

Do ear trumpets work?

You will need:

* **a plastic bottle** • **scissors**

1 Cut the top off a plastic bottle, and hold it against your ear. (Do not push the trumpet all the way into your ear, and make sure no one shouts into the trumpet. It could harm your hearing.)

2 See if you hear better with the ear trumpet. Try bottles of different sizes. The larger the opening, the better your ear trumpet will work.

3 Collect plastic bottles of different sizes to try.

How do speaking tubes work?

You will need:

plastic tubing cut into different lengths
two small funnels to fit the tubing

1 Talk to a friend down your speaking tube.

2 Test whether it matters if the tube is coiled or straight.

3 Test whether sound travels through a long tube as easily as through a shorter one.

4 Make a kink in the tube as a test to see if the sound waves are blocked.

Speaking tubes were used on ships so that the captain could talk to the engine room from the bridge.

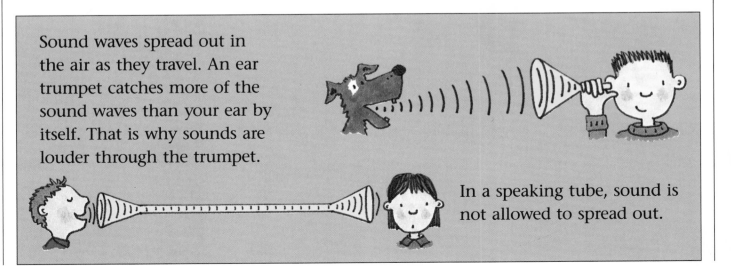

Sound waves spread out in the air as they travel. An ear trumpet catches more of the sound waves than your ear by itself. That is why sounds are louder through the trumpet.

In a speaking tube, sound is not allowed to spread out.

Sound travels through solids

How well does sound travel through solid things?

Handy hearing

1 Carefully put your finger in your ear and lightly scratch your palm. You can hear the sound even if you scratch very gently.

2 Keep scratching your palm gently while you take your finger out of your ear. See how the sound fades out as soon as your finger is out of your ear.

Table tappers

1 Ask a friend to tap the table very gently.

2 Put your ear to the table and listen to the tapping.

Now stand up. Notice how the tapping sound fades or disappears.

Do soft solid things let sound pass through as easily as hard things?

Design an experiment to find out which solid things let sound pass through easily. You could try things like these:

Make a table of your results. Use lots of check marks for things that allow sound to travel through them easily.

Native Americans used to listen for the approach of horses by pressing their ears against the ground. They knew that hard rock transmitted the sound better than soft soil.

19

String telephones

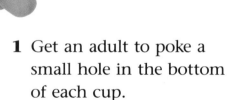

You will need:

- two paper or plastic cups
- A long piece of string
- scissors ◆ a sharp pencil

1 Get an adult to poke a small hole in the bottom of each cup.

2 Thread string through the holes and tie knots in the string to keep it in place.

3 Give one cup to a friend, and take the cups far apart, so that the string is tight. Talk and listen to each other through the string telephone.

What kind of string works best?

Use different kinds of string (or strong yarn) to make string telephones. Experiment to find out which works the best.

What sort of cup works best?

Use different types of cups for the telephone. Ask an adult to make holes in two cans, using a hammer and nail, so that you can try these.

> ### Find out:
>
> what happens if the string goes slack.
>
> what happens if you hold the string.
>
> what happens if you connect three or four string telephones together.

How it works

Your voice makes the container vibrate, which makes . . .

the string vibrate, which makes . . .

the other container vibrate.

Ordinary telephones change sound into electricity, which travels along the wires.

Hearing through water

How well do sounds travel through water?

Noisy seas

Trawlers use sound echoes to find schools of fish.

Dolphins use sound echoes to find their prey.

◄ *Submarines use echoes to find underwater objects.*

1 Put some water in a balloon. Do not fill it too full or it may burst.

2 Listen to a quiet radio through the balloon full of water. For safety, be sure to use a battery-powered radio, not one plugged into an electric socket.

3 Compare the sound through the water with the sound you hear through a balloon full of air to see which of the two materials allows sound waves to pass through it most easily.

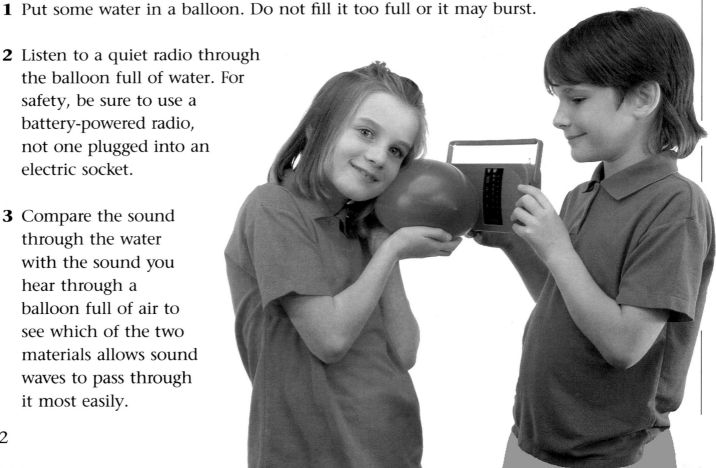

The speed of sound

Sounds travel at different speeds through different materials.

Sound can travel this far in one second:

 1,000 ft. in air

5,000 ft. in water

13,000 ft. in stone

16,400 ft. in steel

Water carries sound so well that a small explosion off South Africa was once heard, using underwater microphones, off the coast of South America, over 4,000 miles away.

Whales keep in contact by singing to each other. Their songs travel hundreds of miles through the sea.

SOUTH AMERICA

SOUTH AFRICA

Listen to underwater sounds using a speaking tube or an ear trumpet.

Blowing high and low notes

1 Practice blowing across the top of juice bottles or soda bottles to make a booming sound.

2 Fill three or four bottles with different amounts of water.

3 Blow across the top of each one.

4 Put them in order from the highest note to the lowest note.

When you blow across the top of the bottle, the air inside the bottle vibrates and makes a sound.

The pitch of the sound depends on the height of the column of air that is vibrating.

A tall column of air gives a low note.

A short column of air gives a high note.

Musical instruments

Make notes of different pitches on a recorder by covering up the holes with your fingers. This alters the length of the tube that the air has to travel through before it escapes through a hole. As more holes are covered, the air vibrates along more of the tube and makes a lower note.

Church organs have tiny pipes for high notes and huge pipes for low notes.

A tuba makes the lowest note of all the brass instruments. Most tubas have between 19 feet and 23 feet of tubing.

short tube = high note

long tube = low note

Blow across the top of a tube like this:

Move the tube up and down in the water, and notice the change in pitch.

String pitch

What changes the sound made by a string?

You will need:

- a table
- some string
- a thick pen or any similar object
- a heavy object to act as a weight

1 Tie the string to one of the table legs.

2 Tie the heavy object to the other end of the string.

3 Put a thick pen under the string on top of the table and pluck the string.

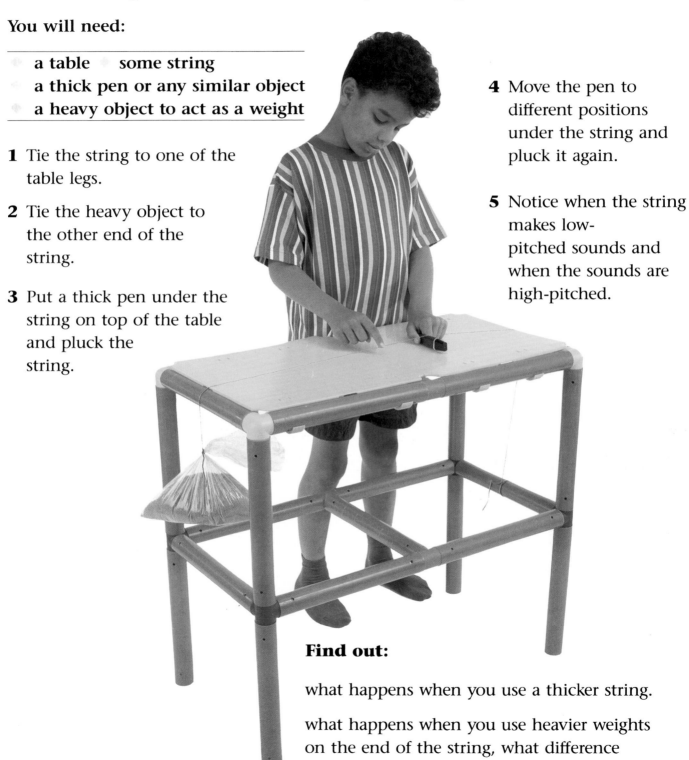

4 Move the pen to different positions under the string and pluck it again.

5 Notice when the string makes low-pitched sounds and when the sounds are high-pitched.

Find out:

what happens when you use a thicker string.

what happens when you use heavier weights on the end of the string, what difference this makes to the pitch of the sound.

Investigate a guitar

The pegs tighten and loosen the strings. Tight strings have a higher pitch than loose ones.

The low notes are played on heavy strings. Wire is wound around the strings to make them heavier.

The high notes are played on lighter, thinner strings.

The wood of a guitar is thin. It vibrates along with the strings and makes the sound louder.

When you press on the **frets** you make the strings shorter, so the notes are higher.

Three things affect the pitch of a string:

High pitch	Low pitch
Short string	Long string
Tight string	Loose string
Light string	Heavy string

Blocking the sound

Which materials would make the best ear protectors?

1 Carefully put a finger in one ear.

2 If you cover the other ear with an empty plastic cup, you can still hear sounds—although not as clearly.

3 Now fill the cup with soft material. Notice how it muffles the sound.

Experiment with different fillings for the ear protector.

This chocolate factory is so noisy that people wear ear protectors at work.

Sounds dangerous
This girl is listening to her personal stereo. She has not heard the car.

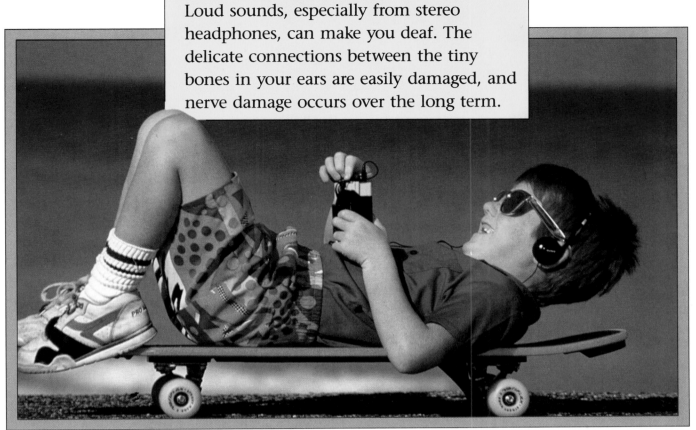

Look after your ears
Loud sounds, especially from stereo headphones, can make you deaf. The delicate connections between the tiny bones in your ears are easily damaged, and nerve damage occurs over the long term.

Creep

Walk

Approach

Think

Lip-read

Deaf people often talk in sign language, using their hands.

Glossary

Cochlea (pronounced COCK-lee-a) The part of the inner ear that changes vibrations into electrical nerve messages.

Eardrum Part of the inner ear. It is made from stretched skin, which vibrates when sound waves hit it.

Echo Sound waves that bounce back off a solid object.

Frets Small metal bars on the neck of a string instrument.

Pitch How high or low a sound is, depending on how many vibrations there are every second. Fast vibrations give high-pitched sounds and slower vibrations give low-pitched sounds.

Sound waves The way in which sound travels through a material, by pressing it together, then pulling it apart.

Source Anything or place from which something comes.

Trawlers Fishing boats that use large nets to catch fish.

Tuning fork A piece of metal, shaped like a fork, that has been measured to a particular size and weight so that it vibrates at a certain speed. This produces an accurate musical pitch.

Vibration Rapid movement back and forth. Vibrations produce sound waves.

Books to read

Darling, David. *Sounds Interesting: The Science of Acoustics.* Experiment! New York: Dillon Press, 1991.

Davies, Kay and Wendy Oldfield. *Sound and Music.* Starting Science. Austin: Steck-Vaughn, 1992.

Friedhoffer, Robert. *Sound.* Scientific Magic; Book 4. New York: Franklin Watts, 1992.

Oxenbury, Helen. *I Hear.* New York: Random, 1986.

Taylor, Barbara. *Sound.* Focus On. New York: Gloucester, 1992.

Chapter Notes

Pages 4-5 These activities concentrate on the importance of having two ears to locate the sound. You may have problems making a very quiet sound to use in the tests. The room in which the hearing tests take place will have to be quiet.

Pages 6-7 Ears are very delicate; the eardrum is a stretched piece of skin that can easily be punctured by sharp objects. Sounds should make the stretched plastic wrap vibrate in the same way as the eardrum.

Pages 8-9 Sound is made by vibrating objects. The faster an object vibrates, the higher the sound it will make. A slowly vibrating object will make a low sound. The pitch of a sound bears no relation to its volume—both high and low sounds can be loud or soft.

Pages 10-11 It is a good idea to make each recording of a sound last at least four seconds. Record sounds you think people will recognize most easily.

Pages 12-13 High-pitched sounds have a short wavelength, so more of them are produced per second. In other words, they have a high frequency. Low-pitched sounds have a longer wavelength and lower frequency.

Slinky springs are a good way of showing how sound waves travel through a material. Although each section of the spring returns to its original position, you can see the waves move along the spring.

Pages 14-15 It is important to understand that sound travels much more slowly than light.

To hear a clear echo, the experiment should be carried out against a blank wall, in quiet surroundings.

Sound can only travel through a material with molecules or atoms that can be made to vibrate.

Space is a vacuum where there is nothing to vibrate, so sounds cannot travel.

Pages 16-17 These pages show that an ear trumpet with a large opening is more effective than one with a smaller opening. That is because the wider opening concentrates vibrations from a wider area. Make sure that the ear trumpet cannot be pushed all the way into the ear.

Pages 18-19 The reason that sound travels better through solids than it does through gases like air is that the molecules of a solid are bound together more tightly than those of a gas. Less energy is therefore lost in the vibration.

Pages 20-21 When testing combinations of materials for the best string telephones, make sure to change only one material at a time; otherwise no fair comparison can be made.

Pages 22-23 Sound travels better in liquids than it does in gases, because the molecules of the liquid are closer together. Sound travels great distances underwater. Sonar uses echoes to locate underwater objects. Dolphins find their prey by the same method. Sometimes they use intense bursts of sound to stun their prey.

Pages 24-25 The reason for the changing pitch of the notes is that the length of the column of air in the bottle determines how long the wavelength of the vibration will be. A shorter wavelength gives a higher pitch and a longer one a lower pitch. The difference in the results when you tap an empty or full bottle is because then the glass (and water) vibrate, not the air.

Pages 26-27 It is a good idea to experiment with old string instruments as well as the weighted string to hear the differences in pitch. Take care to protect the floor and toes from falling weights.

Pages 28-29 Very loud sounds damage the nerves and connections between the bones of the ear. Ear protectors block and absorb sounds before they reach the ear. It is dangerous to listen to a personal stereo when walking or riding bikes, since it does not allow you to hear approaching cars.

Index

Answers to the questions on page 11: 1 false, 2 true, 3 false, 4 true, 5 false, 6 true

Answer to the question on page 14: **B** About four hours